IN THE SAME SERIES

Fiona Benson

———

faber and faber

First published in 2009
by Faber and Faber Ltd
Bloomsbury House
74–77 Great Russell Street
London WC1B 3DA

Typeset by Faber & Faber Ltd
Printed in England by T. J. International Ltd, Padstow, Cornwall

ACKNOWLEDGEMENTS

Thanks are due to the editors of *Addicted to Brightness*, *Areté*, *City
Lighthouse*, *London Review of Books*, *Poetry Review*, *The Red
Wheelbarrow* and *The Times Literary Supplement*, to the Society of
Authors for an Eric Gregory Award and to the Arts and Humanities
Research Council for a vocational studentship. Thanks also to my poetry
teachers, John Burnside, Douglas Dunn, Julie Hanson, Kathleen Jamie,
Don Paterson and Craig Raine; for their support, editorial assistance and
encouragement Matthew Hollis, Peter Straus and David Antoine Williams;
for their love and forbearance, my family and, always, James.

A CIP record for this book
is available from the British Library

ISBN 978-0-571-24995-4

FSC
Mixed Sources
Product group from well-managed
forests and other controlled sources
Cert no. SGS-COC-2482
www.fsc.org
© 1996 Forest Stewardship Council

2 4 6 8 10 9 7 5 3

Contents

Lares

I keep going back to that bird, snagged
by a halter or skein of fibre or yarn
and strung from the gutter of the opposite house
where it quartered the wind, each bead of its spine
and the dead-drop of its skull
lit up against the breeze-block wall,
claws pushed out as if skidding to a halt
while its beak transmitted code.

I say a prayer to you, small ghost,
small noosed spirit of the eaves,
dangling from the prow of the house
singing all four winds, the spindle and pin
and needle and thorn of your hollow bones
riding you on air that is redolent with spores
after the fact of your scavenged heart,
the stolen tissues of your wings.

Emmaus

And if you should forget
walk out across the Hungerford Bridge
where the city falls back

and pylons loom in the dark
like an avenue of silver birch.
Regard the work:

a simple stitch, it heals
the breach of the river, allows passage and pause
to acknowledge our place

beneath this infinite sky
in a wind that knows we are mortal, porous,
a beautiful trick of the light.

Landscape with Harm

We were away on our own, had driven out fast
in a thaw between two storms,
the drifts banked up by the salted road
and the blackthorn's grim wrought-iron

tunnelling us through to this: a derelict barn,
and both of us biting down, latching on,
for a once-off fuck in the dark
that skinned the ridge of my back

and sent you into the white-out to retch,
still buttoning up.
We drove back quiet as the ice resealed,
the red sun level with the fields

and the pitted snow in flames,
closing in on our own small towns,
their lamp-lit rooms, the lane a mile off
where you drop me to walk home.

The Calm

We should have known, the dogs all gone,
and the cats, and the sea sucked back like that,
holding its breath . . . but, hung-over
and at a loose end we were messing around,
prodding at the bellies of the bloat fish that had beached
to make them inflate; there were fleets of them,
liver and tan, their taut skins shimmering, blown.
Jellyfish lay, blistering in the sun.
Translucent crabs surged inland.
About a mile on, that final sign:
sea-urchins nesting in their own dropped spines.

Amandara

Everything is new. Even this morning
women were still planting seedlings between rains,
pressing in orchids with their bare hands;
even the palm-trees, imported from the mainland,
are still surrounded by darker cribs of earth.
We meet and order Singhas. The cicadas are ringing,
shell-pink geckoes twitch on the ceiling,
while bats flicker in at the fringes, picking off moths,
and the workers' dogs pat at bugs and toads
just beyond the light. We're given rice
and steaming curries laced with lemongrass;
the beer-bottles knock against our teeth as we toast.
We can sense them in the dark, exiled but listening,
a stiff, wild current of salt and longing.

Poem for James

Summer; thunder pulsed on the horizon
while hummingbirds slipped through the thickened air
to circle the dropper, sip sugared water,
and I half-waded, half-swam, thigh-deep in pollen,
which rose in a haze from their meadow-grown lawn.
I was straight off the bus in that glaze of heat,
my unwashed skin peppery with sweat,
rucksack, camera, dirt, bearing me down
to the devil. But there you were, waist-deep in saffron,
your long arms folded and every hair on them
glowing like bronze, your red hair on fire
and your dark eyes attentive, though you don't remember,
which is why I'm writing it down, from the goldenrod in bloom
to your nimbus of insects lit by the sun.

Corpo Santo

The ocean surface flexes and I am schooled with the fish,
flanked by the tail and tilt of their angled balance,
the cold intimacies of their flesh.
I could dedicate myself to this:
the pursuit of cadences in salt and warmth
and the sinuous will of this many-ribboned shoal
as it streams into rods of turquoise and gold . . .
I pitch between the water's sides,
its massy, burnished sheets, and am lost to its permissions
and slipways and its taste, as the milky spores
and coral globes of last night's spawning season
thread through my fingers and briefly luminesce,
as if I had somehow found a back door
and, uninvited, entered grace.

Reflex

So you told her
and she didn't miss a beat

kept on talking at the same speed
like that horse in the slaughterhouse

harnessed and hooded
belting for open grass

after the bullet
racing for silence

the green bleed
of meadowsweet and larkspur

before the tongue falls slack and weighty
in the loosened jaw.

Caveat

But consider the cactus:
its thick hide
and parched aspect

still harbour a moist heart;
nick its rind and sap
wells up like sugared milk

from the store of water
held beneath its spines,
its armoury of barbs

and, once a lifetime,
when the hard rains fall
there is this halo of flowers.

First Wife

After the wake you came home. Nothing had changed.
Her trowel stood staked in the rhubarb, squamous with rust,
her boots still flopped where she'd levered them off.
You'd glimpse her face lit over the seed-trays
like a moon in their heaven, spurring them on,
and the bulbs she'd buried pushed up that spring
like they had an appointment with God, all the old battlefields
land-mined and mapped, crocus swathes on the lawn,
four shilling bunches of jonquils, plum blossom
under your bedroom window, peach in her orchard
stomping-ground. Each soft detonation
has its own spindrift of petals and loss,
buds invoking her crab-apple sauce,
scilla primed with the indigo blue of her eyes
of course, of course.
                It'll come back to haunt you,
this other woman kneeling in the grass,
her white blouse glowing at dusk
sowing seed where your first wife left off. You'd reach out
and touch the streak of dirt she's rubbed across her face
if only you could shake the sense you're being watched.
This August you'll twist each tomato off its stem
like a small grenade and weigh it in your palm.
You'll scrape the last of the honey out of its jar
then suck on the spoon as you watch the vacant bird-table
dumb-posted on the lawn, and your new wife
ties raspberry canes and spreads manure, alone.
Nothing will have changed, except your heart,
the pit you swell round, its hurt, its hurt.

Frontiers

I dreamt Margaux had brought back trees from Palestine.
They were in the study but also in the sun, the roof open,
earthed beneath our feet and bearing fruit.
And I thought: how extravagant, how American.
But then I looked up from the desk where I was pinned
and saw their white petals gleaming like pennants,
their pan-flashing leaves channelling the wind
with a sound like uncooked rice being sifted and poured.
And the glamour of that light between the leaves
was like all her other gestures, restless with intelligence,
quick-fingered, wild, stirring at the borders of a splintered world.

Snow-Screens

Last, your father's greenhouse,
his bench of orchids so pale and still
that when it snowed that first light squall
screened itself across their veils,
like ghosts caught falling on the final reel
of an unattended, silent film.
We lay between the benches like stone gisants
watching the dark shake itself out
and neither of us moved or spoke
until the snow began to settle on the glass,
and the gritter came into hearing
toiling up the road, and I shouldered out
into the cold, knowing that a single grain
of warmth, or salt, would melt me whole.

Yellow Room at Arles
from Love-Letter to Vincent

I was back in your yellow room at Arles –
an ochre cube with a bed like a crib
and your paintings all over the walls . . .
But that's not it. I wanted to tell you
that it's so much worse, that the times
of clarity and grace are more and more
remote, that I'm losing ground to the dark.
So I've dug my way back to your golden room,
your wounded girl, your damned and lovely prostitute,
come to sleep it out, teepeed in your scarlet blanket,
with the lamplight dimmed to a red bordello warmth
and a chair against the door. We'll talk or fuck,
or sit and flip cards, whatever you want,
just ferry me through unharmed, uncut.

Prayer

I saw you like a hare, stripped and jugged
in the wine of your own blood, your tail a rudder
steering you through burgundy and juniper,
your eyes gummed shut. Tadpole,

stripling, elver, don't let the dragtides
pull you under, but root in, bed down,
tucked behind my pelvic bone,
rocked in the emptying stoup of my womb.

Sheep

She's lying under a low wind
bedded in mud and afterbirth,
her three dead lambs

knotted in a plastic bag.
Crows have pecked out her arse
and now the hen

that's been circling all morning
tugs at a string of birth-meat
like she's pulling a worm in the yard.

I can't not watch.
I too lay stunned
in my own dirt,

the miscarried child
guttering out,
soaking the mattress in blood.

I was afraid to look down
for what I might see –
a human face, a fist.

Yet once it was done I got up,
gathered my bedding
and walked.

Dogrose Season

That night we left the fire hissing on the beach
and you led us home in the dark through a briar pass
you knew by touch, its flowers ghosted with moths.
I never thought we'd commit you to this earth,
this cliff overlooking sands that we tramped for miles
as the tide pulled back on a bone-yard of shells, and the clouds
swept in, opening and closing their great storm doors
on sun and a sky the deep, psychotic blue
of wild iris. We were walking into our lives.
I come here now to find you in this lifted world;
the clouds speed faster than ever, but you are not
in the salt or the water . . . I wait till the fire goes out
before turning back to the dark, which is suddenly cut
with the scent of dogrose flowers, lighting the path.

Salvage

Dawn floods through
the valley from the east.
A feral rose

that has grown up
through the thorn bush
is caught in its currents –

a single bloom transformed,
become its own lantern
hung above the garden,

radiant, elect,
its ventricles and channels
charged with light,

its scarlet bell streaming,
as if it were Christ's sacred heart
radiating flames,

spilling at the brim
with the jewel-bright pulse
of morning,

already beginning to break apart
with a love of the world
beyond limit, or bearing.